THE TOAD BENEATH THE HARROW

THE TOAD BENEATH THE HARROW

Barbara Uzzell

Illustrated by Mary Griese

ATHENA PRESS
LONDON

To Dorothy

Author's Note

Country, as opposed to county, living and village life has all but disappeared and the associated lifestyles and country characters with it.

The old-type gardeners, cooks, farm labourers, teachers etc. all had wonderful sayings, some having survived several generations.

Although some of these pop up now and again during conversation, most are lost in the hurly-burly of modern life.

Here is a collection of general "country proverbs".

Dip into them and enjoy, read them "slow and sure, like a donkey's gallop."

Foreword

"Tommy? Oh, she was forever put upon – she was like a toad under a harrow."

Thus was described a dear friend of my elderly aunt.

Auntie has many such sayings. Most of her generation used them as part of conversation, without ever realising how very apt they were.

It made me think of other sayings my mother and grandmother used to use and which are unfortunately dying out now and slipping into obscurity with the last of "the village characters and village life". I have captured a few, most from Gloucestershire, but others are country sayings that have colloquial equivalents.

Perhaps if put into print, they will carry forward into the twenty-first century.

So… "trust in the Lord and keep your bowels open!"

Do you know someone who is always put upon by family and friends? Is she "like a toad under a harrow"?

"F.H.B." – Family Hold Back – let visitors eat first!

S omeone, or something that soaks up information, food etc.: "it's like giving a donkey strawberries".

As children, when it was raining and my sister and I were longing to go to the beach we were told to look out for "enough blue sky to make a baby a new bonnet", or "a sailor a pair of trousers". Bliss!

"T.T.T." – Tummy Touch Table – having had a good meal.

For someone who is rebelling against the right thing to do: "well, if you tie yourself to a tree, you must gnaw the bark", or "you made the bed so you must lie on it".

Searching for something tiny on the carpet is like looking for "a flea in a circus", or "a needle in a haystack".

"A whistling woman and a crowing hen, is neither fit for God nor men."

S omebody who is very clumsy is like "a pig with a gun", or "a cow with a cup and saucer".

Someone who thinks themself superior is "very first of May-ish".

H aving just got the butter out of the fridge, is it "as hard as Pharaoh's heart"?

If Mum saw a large-busted lady walking in a very upright manner she would say: "Here she comes, carrying it all before."

My Aunt, having cleaned a mirror or shoes, etc., says she "polished it until it shone like a brass button on a sheep's behind".

When learning that a large garden trough had been taken from a local garden, Auntie remarked: "They will take anything! If it's not too hot, it's not too heavy."

"If wishes were horses, beggars would ride."

When one likes the good things of life, but can't really afford them, it's "having champagne tastes with a beer pocket".

Having spent hours in the bathroom getting dolled up, at my appearance, I was told: "Here you are, all dressed up and nowhere to go."

If I asked my mother how much things cost, she would say: "Money and good words," or "Umpence ha'penny."

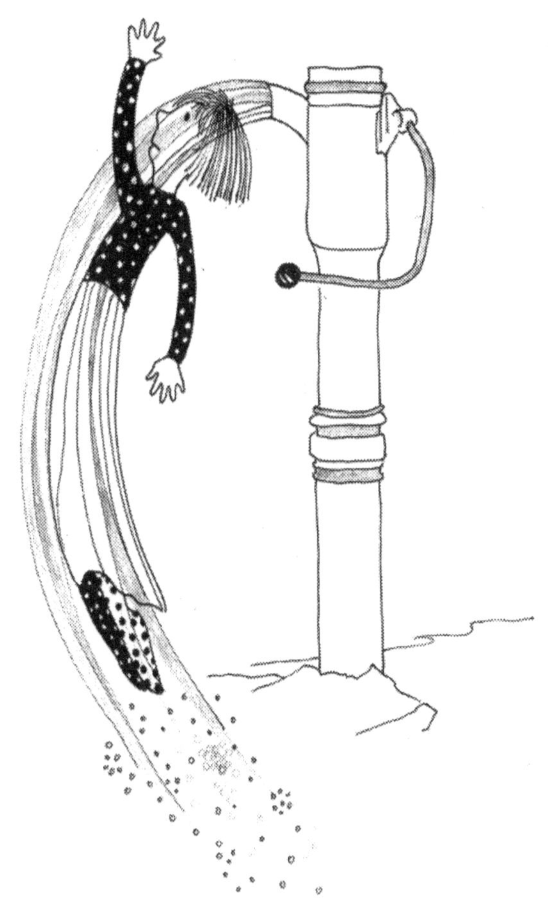

Seeing a very skinny person, Mum's comment would be: "Good gracious, she's like a yard of paralysed pump water!"

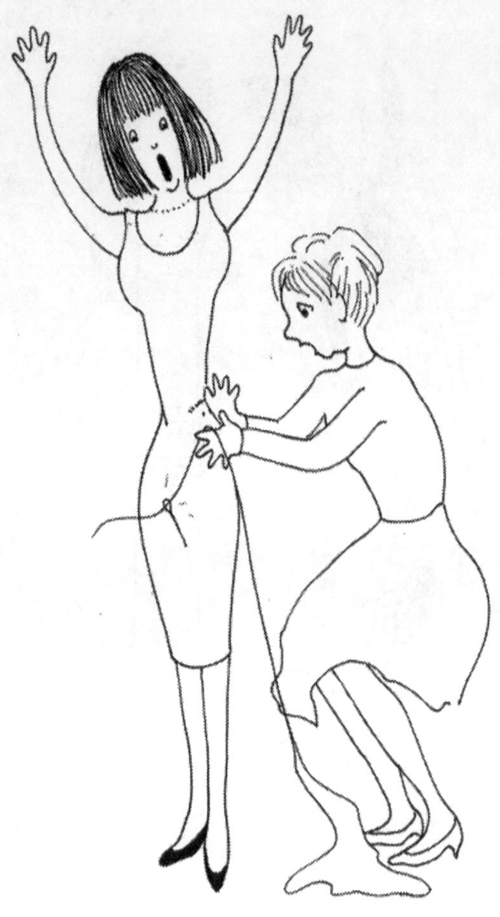

Having bought a new jacket or dress and the seams split, or the buttons dropped off, Mum would say: "A red hot needle and a waxed thread were used to sew this."

S eeing an ominous black cloud, Auntie would remark: "Just look at that 'Black Harry'," or my mum would say: "It looks black over Bill's mother's."

Having made that final decision, just trust in the Lord and keep your bowels open.

Having problems? Need to share them, talk to someone? After all, "two heads are better than one, even if they are sheep's heads".

My dear grandmamma, on a wet blustery day, after hanging out the washing would say: "We must watch for the weather and fly for the clothes."

A good strong cup of tea is "tea so strong you could trot a mouse across it".

Is there someone you know who "worries herself into fiddle strings"?

Monday morning feeling, nothing going right? Are you "all over the place like Brown's cows"?

After being cheeky to her dad when young,
Auntie was told: "Your tongue will lick your
back one day, young lady."

If I protested at the amount of food on my plate, as a youngster, Mum would say: "Eat what you can and can what you can't."

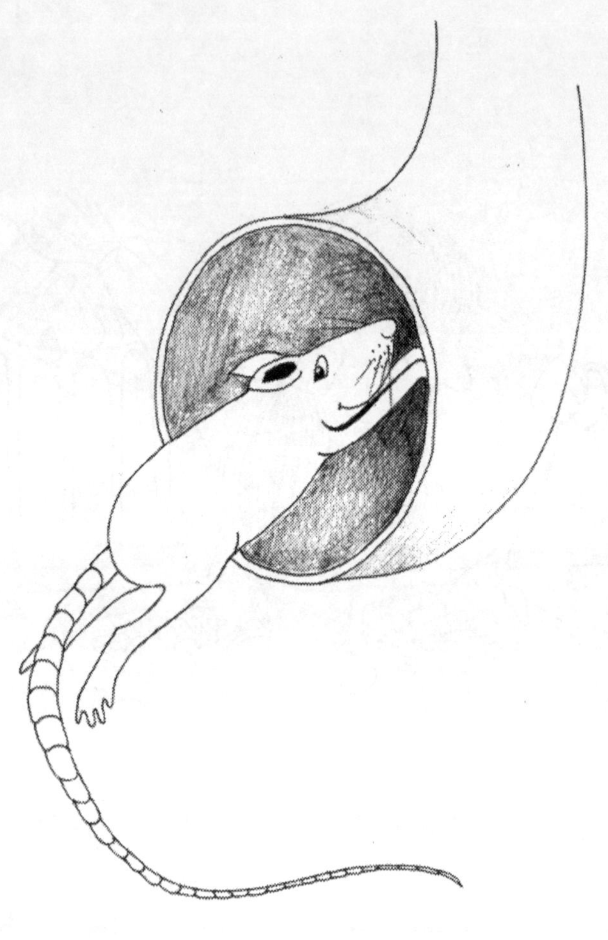

If you see someone you don' t wish to meet, do you run "like a grease spot down a rainbow", or "a rat up a drainpipe"?

Ever been had and bought a "pig in a poke"?

Muttering about someone after an argument:
"Oh! Let 'em went!"

Of a friend who called a spade a spade: "Oh, she doesn't peel any eggs!"

"Washed and polished like a herring's eyeball."

A person who is a bit parsimonious, afraid of spending money, is told: "Shrouds don't have pockets."

H aving spent more than is sensible: "Money goes like butter in the sun."

Having noticed a particularly furtive alliance at a house in the road, Auntie wryly observed: "He's just turned up, they're having a dark half-hour."

Of someone who was always spending, Auntie would say: "Ah, they who have orchards can eat apples."

Of an unfeeling and careless character: "Ah well, the black ox hasn't trod on her feet yet!"

About a busy person always rushing around: "Like a pea on a skillet!"

Family Favourites

My Uncle always collected any unused cutlery or plates after a meal. They were "T.G.s" – Thank God they don't have to be washed!

When dressed up to go out you are "dressed up to the nines".

"F.T.B." – Full To Bursting.

"Be good, sweet maid, and let who will be clever."

On hearing a crash from the kitchen, Mum would say: "Save the pieces!"

Having asked what was for lunch, it was always "bread and pullit"!

About a person who looks down and dejected: "a ha'porth of God help"; "hopeless and helpless"; "sawney".

"God helps those who help themselves."

A place for everything and everything in its place.

Having made a particularly good sponge cake, it was "light as air at early morn".

"Slow and sure, like a donkey's gallop."

"Never trouble trouble till trouble troubles you."

"A fool is only a fool when he thinks he's a fool."

"Give a penny, spend a penny a penny saved."

"Nothing ventured, nothing gained."

Sitting in a darkening room, Auntie would say: "Oh, put the light on, it's dark like a blind man's holiday!"

"Better the day, better the deed."

My friend's mother, if surprised by something, would say: "God bless us and save us, Old Mrs Davies, I never knew herrings were fish!"

My mum, if things were difficult or too heavy for her, said: "I ouds't if I coulds't but I cassn't!"

And if she had her hands full, she'd say: "Hold this while I fetch a policeman."

Sheepish Sayings

Someone who is deceptive is "a wolf in sheep's clothing", or "pulling the wool over your eyes".

A flirt, or just funny – "making sheep's eyes".

www.ingramcontent.com/pod-product-compliance
Lightning Source LLC
Chambersburg PA
CBHW051418250726
48655CB00003B/1115